# TAKE MORE JOY

# TAKE MORE JOY

Jean Louise Smith

ST. MARY'S COLLEGE PRESS • WINONA, MINNESOTA

To my niece, Sarah

*Cover*
IN THE HAMMOCK
by Waldo Peirce
oil
Courtesy, Midtown Galleries
New York

ISBN 0-88489-054-6

Library of Congress Card Catalog #73-87023

# CONTENTS

1 COME, LISTEN, LOOK . . . . . . . . . . . . . . . . . 1

2 COME, CELEBRATE . . . . . . . . . . . . . . . . 25

3 ENJOY SHAPES, COLORS, SOUNDS . . . . . . . 49

4 COME ALIVE . . . . . . . . . . . . . . . . . . . . . 65

5 FULFILLMENT . . . . . . . . . . . . . . . . . . . . 81

# 1
# COME, LISTEN, LOOK!

SEINE AT ARGENTEUIL<
by Pierre Auguste Renoir
French, 1873, oil on canvas
Bequest of Winslow B. Ayer
Courtesy, Portland Art Museum

# Wonder

Wonder comes in at least nine varieties, according to one large dictionary. Any one of the nine definitions of wonder is in itself wonderful—at different times each can be meaningful for you as a person.

If you are wondering *about* something, you are perhaps "thinking or speculating curiously" about how that something began, or what its history is. For example, you might wonder what first brought the early settlers to the town where you live.

If you are doubting, you might say, "I wonder if the pioneers had time to enjoy life. They had to work so hard!" So it goes—*wonder* is a many-faceted word.

But the definition of wonder that most of us think of first is a *feeling* that fills us with "admiration, amazement, and awe." This is the kind of wonder that brings joy and added dimensions to life.

To wonder at the wind tossing tree branches, blowing great, billowing, white and silver clouds across a blue sky, stretches both the eye and the imagination. To lie out on the beach and watch a boat scudding along with the wind puffing its sails is to feel a kind of admiration for this invisible force so important to man.

WOMAN BEFORE AN
AQUARIUM >
by Henri Matisse
French, 1921, oil on canvas
Helen Birch Bartlett Memorial
Collection
Courtesy, The Art Institute
of Chicago

2

Or take a common, everyday wonder. Bake a loaf of bread, or gather garden flowers for a living-room bouquet, or watch children at play, or just dream for a moment while you look at fish in an aquarium. Each of these simple activities has its own wonder, too often passed by because most of us have forgotten to take more than the merest fleeting joy in the fragrance of baking bread, in the sight of a charming bouquet, or in the delicate iridescent stripes, spots, and colors of small fish. Even the common dandelion may evoke admiration, as it did for Jean François Millet, a French artist of the last century. In the hundred years since Millet's death, what has happened to make us dull to simple beauties? Has our capacity to wonder at everyday things shifted completely to an admiration of complex technological exploits such as moon landings?

For most of us today, wonder has to be cultivated and nurtured. This takes time and attention—looking and thinking. Wonder is an experience that needs to be invited. To invite wonder is one way to take a step toward more joy!

DANDELIONS <
by Jean Francois Millet
French, 1814-1875
pastel
Shaw Collection
Courtesy, Museum of Fine Arts
Boston

## Take More Joy in Nature

Is modern man dying of boredom because he finds life so mechanized that vast areas of it are monotonous in their repetition? Tasks in the home, done over and over; jobs in the factory, at a trade, at an office desk—do they lull workers into a kind of numbness that makes them continuously weary, irritable, and empty? . . .

Children are better at taking joy than adults. They find and care for pets, go hiking, cook out of doors, roam and play in nature centers and parks. Nevertheless, people of all ages who have discovered ways to take more joy find time for it. Those happy ones tell us that the search for new joy requires an open-mindedness, an expectancy that it will be found, even in the busiest of lives. They find joy in an invitation to look around them in city and country.

Those who have never found either joy or solace in nature might begin by looking not for the *joy they can get*, but for the *joy that is there* amid those portions of the earth man has not yet entirely pre-empted for his own use. And perhaps when they have become aware of joy in other creatures they will achieve joy themselves, by sharing it.

THE BEST NATURE WRITINGS
OF JOSEPH WOOD KRUTCH<
by Joseph Wood Krutch
excerpt
William Morrow and Company, Inc.
1970
Used by permission

DUCK>
by Francois Pompon
bronze
Gift of Abby Aldrich Rockefeller
Collection, The Museum of
Modern Art
New York

O world! What pictures and what harmonies are thine!
The clouds are rich and dark, the air serene.

There's joy in the mountains;
There's life in the fountains;
Small clouds are sailing,
Blue sky prevailing;
The rain is over and gone!

"THE ADIRONDACKS" <
by Ralph Waldo Emerson
excerpt

"WRITTEN IN MARCH" <
by William Wordsworth
excerpt

CHILDREN ON THE SEASHORE >
by Pierre Auguste Renoir
French, 1841-1919
Bequest of John T. Spaulding
Courtesy, Museum of Fine Arts
Boston

8

# People and Parks

If you live in the city, a park is for walking or strolling. A park means a chance to sit on a bench or loll on the grass, have a picnic, play ball, walk your dog, fly a kite. Even in the midst of great, crowded cities, such as New York, Boston, or Los Angeles, large tracts of land are preserved as parks, even though the monetary value of that land may be astronomically high. Yes, parks are important to city people.

Parks are also important for people who live in small towns and villages, but for different reasons. A ballgame, a band concert, a barbecue is still a fairly common sight on summer evenings in the parks of our towns and villages. With a bit of luck, a tourist in New England may come upon an auction on a village green. Or on a hot Sunday afternoon, the green may be deserted except for a handful of children who are wanting to stir up some action or create a bit of fun. But once the sun sets, the park begins to come to life. Friends gather, drifting from the shelter of front porches, pulling up in cars if they live some distance away. The high school band assembles, tunes up, and a concert begins. In rural places, parks are for sociability.

What, indeed, would people do without parks?

SPRING IN CENTRAL PARK <
by Adolf (Arthur) Dehn
American, 1895-1968
watercolor
Fletcher Fund, 1941
The Metropolitan Museum of Art
New York

11

Little park that I pass through,
I carry off a piece of you
Every morning hurrying down
To my work-day in the town;
Carry you for country there
To make the city ways more fair.
I take your trees,
And your breeze,
Your greenness,
Your cleanness,
Some of your shade, some of your sky,

"ELLIS PARK" >
by Helen Hoyt

12

Some of your calm as I go by;
Your flowers to trim
The pavements grim;
Your space for room in the jostled street
And grass for carpet to my feet.
Your fountains take and sweet bird calls
To sing me from my office walls.
All that I can see
I carry off with me.
But you never miss my theft,
So much treasure you have left.
As I find you, fresh at morning,
So I find you, home returning
Nothing lacking from your grace.
All your riches wait in place
For me to borrow
On the morrow.
Do you hear this praise of you
Little park that I pass through?

## Nature Has Many Meanings

To learn to see the out-of-doors with the artists' eyes is to find more joy! The French artist Renoir found joy in the beauty of sunlight on water, sand, and meadow. The people in his paintings show enjoyment of the world they and he lived in. Millet, on the other hand, painted more somber scenes—often of peasants laboring in the fields. But he did some joyous paintings also, such as "Dandelions," in which every stick and stone, every stalk and flower, blade of grass and leaf stands alone as a piece of beauty!

All too often we visit woods, seashore, and mountains only once a year, during our annual vacation from work. Our British friends go "on holiday" in a fashion we may well envy. On weekends—particularly on the longer Bank Holiday weekends—they pack their rucksacks, dress informally, and crowd on buses and trains to head for the country or the seashore to fish, swim, take a walking tour, or just sit in the sun. They spread out over their small island to revel in whichever natural setting they happen to enjoy most.

IN THE MEADOW <
by Pierre Auguste Renoir
French, 1841-1919
oil on canvas
Bequest of Samuel A. Lewisohn
The Metropolitan Museum of Art
New York

15

The little cares that fretted me,
    I lost them yesterday
Among the fields above the sea,
    Among the winds at play;
Among the lowing of the herds,
    The rustling of the trees,
Among the singing of the birds,
    The humming of the bees.
The foolish fears of what may happen—
    I cast them all away
Among the clover-scented grass,
    Among the new-mown hay;
Among the husking of the corn
    Where drowsy poppies nod,
Where ill thoughts die and good are born,
    Out in the fields with God.

Author Unknown <

CROQUET SCENE >
by Winslow Homer
1866, oil on canvas
Friends of American Art Collection
Courtesy, The Art Institute
of Chicago

I have found that walking stimulates observation and opens one's eyes to movements and appearances in earth and sky, which ordinarily escape attention. The constant change of landscape which attends even the slow progress of a loitering gait puts one on the alert for discoveries of all kinds, and prompts one to suspect every leafy cover and to peer into every wooded recess with the expectation of surprising nature . . . in the moment of uncovered loveliness. . . .

When I reached the end of my walk, and paused for a moment before retracing my steps, I was conscious of the inexhaustible richness of the world through which I had come; a thousand voices had spoken to me, and a thousand sights of wonder moved before me; I was awake to the universe which most of us see only in broken and unintelligent dreams. . . . I began to wonder how many of those now long asleep really saw or heard this great glad world of sun and summer!

UNDER THE TREES
AND ELSEWHERE >
by Hamilton Wright Mabie
excerpts

18

Who has not heard, amid the heat and din of cities,.the voice of the sea striking suddenly into the hush of thought its penetrating note of mystery and longing? Then work and the fever which goes with it vanished on the instant, and in the crowded street or narrow room there rose the vision of unbroken stretches of sky, free winds, and the surge of the unresting waves. . . .

The sea speaks to the imagination as no other aspect of the natural world does, because of its vastness . . . and overwhelming power. . .

It is because the sea preserves its secret that it sways our imagination so royally, and holds us by an influence which never loosens its grasp. Again and again we return to it, spent and worn, and it refills the cup of vitality. . . . Facing its unbroken solitudes, the limitations of habit and thought become less obvious; we escape the monotony of a routine, which blurs the senses and makes the spirit less sensitive to the universe about it. Life becomes free and plastic once more; a deep consciousness of its inexhaustibleness comes over us and recreates hope, vigour, and imagination.

There is pleasure in the pathless woods,
There is a rapture on the lonely shore,
There is society where none intrudes
By the deep Sea, and music in its roar;
I love not Man the less, but nature more,
From these our interviews, in which I steal
From all I may be, or have been before,
To mingle with the Universe, and feel
What I can ne'er express, yet can not all conceal.

"THE SEA">
by Lord Byron
excerpt

BOATING <
by Edouard Manet
French, 1832-1883
oil on canvas
Bequest of Mrs. H. O. Havemeyer,
The H. O. Havemeyer Collection
The Metropolitan Museum of Art
New York

21

Glory be to God for dappled things—
    For skies of couple-colour as a brinded cow;
      For rose-moles all in stipple upon trout
      that swim;
Fresh-firecoal chestnut-falls; finches' wings;
    Landscape plotted and pieced—fold, fallow,
    and plough;
    And all trades, their gear and tackle and trim.
All things counter, original, spare, strange;
    Whatever is fickle, freckled (who knows how?)
      With swift, slow, sweet, sour; adazzle, dim;
He fathers-forth whose beauty is past change:
      Praise him.

"PIED BEAUTY" >
by Gerard Manley Hopkins
excerpt

THE NORTHWEST WIND <
by Charles Harold Davis
oil on canvas
Walter H. Schulze Memorial
Collection
Courtesy, The Art Institute
of Chicago

# 2
# COME, CELEBRATE!

RAINBOW BRIDGE<
by Mirtala Bentov
bronze
Courtesy, Pucker/Safrai Gallery
Boston

## Come, Celebrate!

Since we prize life so much, just being alive is one reason to celebrate. And then there are those special things: joy of family and friends, times for loafing, books to treasure, music to enjoy and to dance to, holidays and holy days.

When celebration comes spontaneously it is like a great big WOW! It happens whenever joy breaks over a person or event with no advance notice.

There are also celebrations that are chosen, carefully planned, and carried out with the realization that now, on this particular occasion, we will celebrate.

When did you last blow bubbles? Fly a kite? Stretch out on the grass in a park or field? Pick a bouquet of field daisies?

Do you think that things like these are for children only? Sure of this?

Look who's blowing the bubble in Jean Baptiste Chardin's painting!

Watch a group of people of various ages enjoying themselves. The grownups are as eager to enter into the fun as the children—glad of the chance to unwind.

BLOWING BUBBLES <
by Jean Baptiste Simeon Chardin
French, 1699-1779
oil on canvas
Catherine D. Wentworth Fund
The Metropolitan Museum of Art
New York

27

So . . . *down* with any adult notion that taking part in the celebrations of life is childish. Respond freely to expressions of joy and praise in contemporary worship. Clap the hands! Tap the feet! Sing out! *Down* with the idea that only children should skip rope, run across a field or go to circuses!

Any time is well spent when it is used for taking joy.

Youth is sounding a clarion note these days to remind their elders to *feel* life more and find natural ways of releasing tensions.

So *up* with bubbles and kites and trips to the beach. *Up* with enjoyment of beautiful common things like black-eyed susans, the liquid song of meadowlarks, a friend's smile!

Times of being idle—of doing nothing much—are really celebrations of the self's aliveness. A joyful ceasing of work for a long or short time is an unwinding of tension. Gradually one becomes aware of the sweet smells of the meadow, the song of birds and experiences of loving and being loved. At such times we are truly aware and alive: celebrating. As Mary Ryan says in *We're All in This Together*, experiences such as swimming, walking in a beautiful place, creating something and seeing it is good, discovering and delighting in the beauty of nature

STILTS, NO. 2>
by Leona Pierce
1951, woodcut, in black and red
Collection, The Museum of
Modern Art
New York

or a work of art or a person, all serve to release us, help us to reach out beyond ourselves. This reaching out is a "more than I" that opens out to a sense of the ultimate—even to God.

The sense of the self is celebrated whenever one reaches out to another, for a shared experience between two persons creates a bridge between them. Across this bridge flow acts of giving, sharing, and mutual joy. Each self becomes a larger self and finds a new interest in a more inclusive "we."

## The Symmetry of a Rich Life

The law of association weaves a man's life after a time into a rich and varied texture, in which the sober threads of care and work are interwoven with the soft hues of love and the splendid dyes of imagination; feelings, thoughts, actions are no longer detached and isolated; they are blended together into the fullness and symmetry of a rich life. One's toil gathers sweetness from the thought of those to whose comfort it ministers; one's friends stand for . . . achievement; and one's life ceases to be a single strain, and becomes a harmony of many chords, each suggesting and deepening the melody of every other.

"SONG OF MYSELF">
by Walt Whitman
excerpt

MY STUDY FIRE<
Hamilton Wright Mabie
excerpt

BOYS IN A PASTURE>
by Homer Winslow
American
Charles Henry Hayden Fund
Courtesy, Museum of Fine Arts
Boston

30

I loaf and invite my soul,
I lean and loaf at my ease,
Observing a spear of summer grass.

## People Are Worth Celebrating!

There is something very special about a certain small leather-bound volume which I acquired sometime ago. I came upon the *Imitation of Christ* by Thomas à Kempis at a rummage sale. I had long wanted to add the title to my personal library, and there it was, in excellent condition!

Several days went by before I found time to look at my purchase carefully and discover the unexpected pleasure and delight of meeting its former owner. This followed a lingering enjoyment of the book itself: the leather binding in soft slightly faded rose, worthy of the gold embellishments. The cover had a certain patina that in no way marred it: a scattering of dots or small spots, possibly made by water, which created a deep shade of rose here and there.

When I turned the cover to see the inside lining, to my delight it was an even darker rose than the outer cover. This deep mulberry color was elegantly watermarked in a swirling pattern. In the tiniest of gold type the designer's name had been embossed at the very bottom of the inside front cover. This somehow added to the importance and value of my small book.

Another turn of the page revealed the flyleaf, on which was written the name of the owner: Emilie L. Weiskotten. Emilie had evidently catalogued her personal library, for neatly inscribed at the foot of the page was the number 512.

Turning then to the title page brought yet another delight! Closely written in old-fashioned spidery handwriting were the names of fourteen women below the message: "To Emilie, one whom we all love." Several were names seldom heard these days: Otylia, Nettie, Hermine, Carrie, Lizzie, and Hilda.

Who were these women? Members of a faithful Sunday school class? A study group? Obviously not a bridge club or cooking class! In fancy I have come to think of that little group as fellow seekers after truth, with Emilie as their loved and respected leader.

As I turned the pages, two other clues to Emilie as a person fell out in the form of two small greeting cards. One, in German, had on it the verse "The Lord is faithful; he will strengthen you and guard you from evil." This was beautifully printed below a delicate pastel-colored floral circlet. On the back of the card was a personal message, also in German.

The second card, in black and white, contained a Christmas greeting: a somewhat sentimental picture of the Madonna and Child, with a bit of verse under it. On the back, Emilie's friend Hermine had written a note that began "Dear Lady." It was a warm greeting from her old friend with best wishes for a safe journey and a pleasant visit. So Emilie traveled! Perhaps she had taken the small volume of the *Imitation of Christ* with her and had slipped the Christmas card in among its pages.

The only marked passage in the book gave an interesting insight into Emilie's character, for it was a comment on *things* and the need for man to control them rather than for things to control man. It ended, "The more a man suffers himself to be hindered and distracted by things, the more he is moved by them."

Emilie must have pondered this idea and wondered if she fully agreed with Thomas à Kempis. Certainly, her more than five hundred books were things that brought her joy and pleasure—worthy distractions. For her, the world of books and the people who use them were good to know.

Emilie and her friends reach across the decades to all of us who treasure books as companions that enrich the mind and spirit.

WOMAN AND CHILD
PLAYING DOMINOES >
by Pierre Auguste Renoir
French, 1841-1919
Courtesy, Museum of Fine Arts
Boston

Great friendship is delight: a hyphen between
two minds, a bridge between two wills, a selfless
joy in the loving, giving, sharing, daring life, where
two outgivings merge into one, two people lose their
small "I" and find new interest in a large "you."

THE BOOK OF FRIENDSHIP<
by Elizabeth Selden
excerpt
Houghton Mifflin Company
Boston, 1947
Used by permission

PICKING FLOWERS>
by Pierre Auguste Renoir
French, 1841-1919
Bequest of Hannah Marcy Edwards
in memory of her mother, Juliana
Cheney Edwards
Courtesy, Museum of Fine Arts
Boston

# Things Worth Celebrating

There are quiet celebrations that come almost daily. They are *there*, although we do not always recognize their presence.

And then there are circuses. They are the WOW! celebrations. "Damn everything but the circus," the poet e. e. cummings wrote. No mere cussing, this; but if not, what is it? S. Helen Kelley thought about it and wrote an interpretation:

damn everything
that is grim, dull, motionless, unrisking,
inward turning,
 damn everything
that won't get into the circle,
that won't enjoy
that won't throw its heart
 into the tension,
  surprise,
  fear
  and delight of the circus,
  the round world,
the full existence . . .

by S. Helen Kelley >
Used by permission of S. Helen Kelley
and Corita Prints

INVITATION TO THE SIDE-
SHOW (LA PARADE) <
by Georges Seurat
French, 1859-1891
oil on canvas
Bequest of Stephen C. Clark
The Metropolitan Museum of Art
New York

39

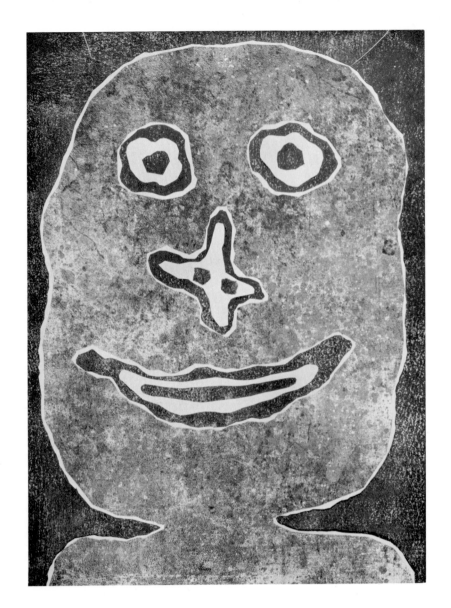

What is a smile?
It's all mouth!
It's eyes, big as can be!
It's a wrinkled-up nose!
A smile takes up a whole face—
Makes a shape that breaks up into a hundred
    wrinkles that say, "I'm happy;
How about *you*?"
A person can smile all by himself,
But it's more enjoyable to smile with another—
To find quiet joy in sharing a sight, an idea,
    or a moment of feeling close.
A smile is to take more joy.
*That's* what a smile is!

THE SMILE (LE SOURIRE, I) <
by Jean Dubuffet
1961, cut and pasted lithographed
papers
Gift of Mr. and Mrs. Ralph F.
Colin in honor of Rene
d'Harnoncourt
Collection, The Museum of
Modern Art
New York

In his book *Feast of Fools*, the contemporary theologian Harvey Cox suggests that affluent Western man has gained the world at a great cost: the cost of "impoverishment of the vital elements of his life." These, he says, are *festivity* and *fantasy*.

Let's have fun
 let's find joy in life
and love and hope,
Shout in our hearts
 on the feast of the Sun
that Son, our brother, is here
 in love. let's have fun
 with flowers and laughter
and each other and everyone.
let's delight in the small happenings,
smiles and understanding,
 peaceful moments and giving.
 let's celebrate every open mind
and heart and small signs
of love that slip away so fast
if we aren't looking.
 let's rejoice we are, and the
 daily thin thread of living
will be part of all
 the world's tomorrows.

More simply stated, but along the same line of thought, is the list of "My Twelve Loveliest Things (People Not Counted)" made by a young Scots girl:

The scrunch of dry leaves as you walk
    through them
The feel of clean clothes
Water running into the bath
The cold of ice cream
Cool wind on a hot day
Climbing up and looking back
Honey in your mouth
Smell of a drugstore
Hot water bottle in bed
Babies smiling
The feeling inside when you sing
Baby kittens.

## Picnics

What makes a picnic?
A sunny day
A few friends
A lovely place out of doors
Some food that has been gathered up into a basket
These are and always have been the ingredients for a picnic!

In his painting "The Picnic," Jerome Thompson included all of those essentials: a sunny spring day, a group of friends in a meadow by a river, and a basket of food. The picnickers in this painting, done a hundred years ago, could be of our own time: the women in long, full skirts, the men with long hair, mustaches, and beards, music being piped by one of the young men for the pleasure of his friends.

A picnic is a celebration of joy—joy in the blending of friendship and nature, in the breaking of bread together.

Thank God for picnics!

THE PICNIC<
by Jerome Thompson
American, 1812-1886
oil on canvas
Courtesy, M. H. De Young
Memorial Museum

## Celebrating Holidays and Holy Days

Beginning with New Year's Day and ending with Christmas, regularly designated holidays mark the year. Scattered over the twelve months are the holy days and seasons: Lent and Easter, Christmas, saints' days; Passover, Rosh Hashanah, Tabernacles, Purim; Sunday and the Sabbath marking each week.

Then there are the personal celebrations: birthdays, anniversaries, ceremonies of baptism, bar mitzvah, marriage. So it goes. It seems that we might be celebrating joyfully many times each year.

But do we? Are we losing our touch for meaningful celebrations in the rush of today's living?

Who and what in your life determines how you celebrate holidays and holy days? Check over these questions—they may suggest further questions that you can supply:

Was the celebration creative? Did it draw on individual talents? Were some gifts homemade? Was some food cooked at home, or was everything "store bought"? Did members of the household all have a part in the preparations? Was a visitor or unattached person included to share in the event? Was the emphasis on persons: feelings of warmth and friendship, appreciation of each other as well as of the group or family? Did you come to the end of the day

THANKSGIVING >
by Doris Lee
1935, oil on canvas
Mr. and Mrs. Frank G. Logan
Courtesy, The Art Institute
of Chicago

46

(or season) feeling more fulfilled and enriched? More appreciative of persons and of life's values? More aware of the intangibles that are what a good life is all about? Did the intangibles—the values—outweigh the material ingredients of gift-giving, food, the display of possessions and things?

# 3

# ENJOY SHAPES, COLORS, SOUNDS

FISH RIDE<
by Robert Vickrey
1972, tempera
Private Collection
Courtesy, Midtown Galleries
New York

## Looking at Common Things

Claude Monet, the French Impressionist, must have spent hundreds of hours observing haystacks, for in all seasons, all kinds of weather, and at all times of day he went out to the fields to paint them. It is probable that he made well over a hundred haystack paintings, some of which were done in early morning light, others at noon, mid-afternoon, twilight—haystacks seen through rain or drenched in sunlight.

Monet was also fascinated with waterlilies: he painted them countless times. One of these paintings, in the Museum of Fine Arts, Boston, is a huge panorama of waterlilies in a quiet pool. The rainbow colors of the delicately shaded pink and white blossoms, with their huge leaves floating flat on the water, are heightened by the sunlight playing over them.

To look carefully at Monet's paintings of haystacks and waterlilies is to begin to realize that most of us are poor observers. We seldom take time to look lingeringly at a scene or at a single object like a flower or a leaf, and to appreciate and enjoy its shape, colors, and relationships to other objects.

What an imaginative observer is Naum Gabo,

TWO HAYSTACKS >
by Claude Monet
French, 1840-1926
oil on canvas
Mr. and Mrs. Lewis L. Coburn
Courtesy, The Art Institute
of Chicago

50

a contemporary artist! Did he, perhaps, have a cobweb in mind when he created "Linear Construction in Space, Number 4"? With plastic and stainless steel this artist is able to form shapes that are as transparent and magnificently delicate as a cobweb. He is one who can look at the commonplace and, letting his imagination play upon it, create objects of sheer beauty.

Artists can help the rest of us to be better observers when they show us that white is made up of many colors; that objects look different at various times of day and in various lights; that shapes and textures are important. One does not have to be an artist to enjoy seeing a haystack, a flower, or a cobweb with the sun shining through it.

Try this to test your sense of observation and enjoyment: Find two pictures you like very much. Put them where you will see them and then look at them carefully from time to time. After two weeks replace them with two other pictures that you think are better than the first set of pictures.

Live with these for two weeks. Decide which two pictures you really like best, and *why*.

## Thoughts on Wonder

The man who cannot wonder, who does not habitually wonder and worship . . . is but a pair of spectacles, behind which there is no eye.

Wonder results when a person can feel alive, can reach out to all kinds of things and events in interest and responsiveness. You have to be aware to wonder. Passive man cannot wonder.

Finally, brethren, whatsoever things are true, whatsoever things are honest, whatsoever things are just, whatsoever things are pure, whatsoever things are lovely, whatsoever things are of good report; if there be any virtue, and if there be any praise, think on these things.

SARTOR RESARTUS<
by Thomas Carlyle
excerpt

Author Unknown<

PHILIPPIANS 4:8<

LINEAR CONSTRUCTION
IN SPACE
NUMBER 4>
by Naum Gabo
1957
Collection of the Whitney Museum
of American Art

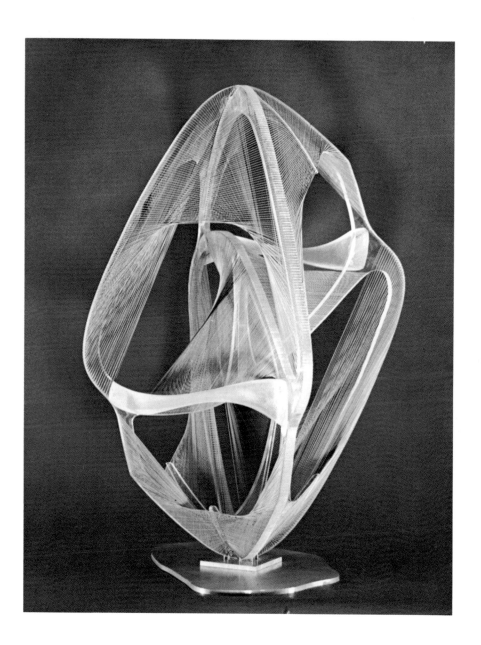

What is this life if, full of care,
We have no time to stand and stare.

No time to stand beneath the boughs
And stare as long as sheep or cows.

No time to see, when woods we pass,
Where squirrels hide their nuts in grass.

No time to turn at Beauty's glance,
And watch her feet, how they can dance.

No time to wait till her mouth can
Enrich that smile her eyes began.

A poor life this if, full of care,
We have no time to stand and stare.

"LEISURE">
by William Henry Davies
excerpt

FLOWERS AND A BOWL
OF FRUIT<
by Paul Gauguin
French, 1848-1903
canvas board
Bequest of John T. Spaulding
Courtesy, Museum of Fine Arts
Boston

I have a little shadow
    that goes in and out with me,
And what can be the use
    of him is more than I can see.
He is very, very like me
    from the heels up to the head;
And I see him jump before me,
    when I jump into my bed.

The funniest thing about him
    is the way he likes to grow—
Not at all like proper children,
    which is always very slow;
For he sometimes shoots up taller
    like an India rubber ball,
And he sometimes gets so little
    that there's none of him at all.

· · · · · · · · · · · · · · · · · · · · · · · ·

One morning very early,
    before the sun was up,
I rose and found the shining dew
    on every buttercup;
But my lazy little shadow,
    like an arrant sleepyhead,
Had stayed at home behind me
    and was fast asleep in bed.

"MY SHADOW" >
by Robert Louis Stevenson

CARRI AND COCOA<
by Robert Vickrey
tempera
Courtesy, Midtown Galleries
New York

59

## The Old Music Teacher

When we read that our old music teacher was to be interviewed on television, our first reaction was "Heavens, is Doc Jones still alive?"

He was indeed very much alive, at the age of ninety. Furthermore, he came on strong and clear, speaking up for Schubert, Bach, and the rest of that distinguished older crowd. He put in a plug for Prokofiev and some of the other moderns too!

Many of us who had taken Doc Jones's course, Music Appreciation I, were warmed by the sight and sound of his appearance on television. We got out the textbook he had written, dusted off our recordings of the "Three B's," and began to enjoy life a little more. Doc Jones somehow, during decades of teaching, had communicated his own enthusiasm for enjoyment of music.

It would seem impossible for any of Doc Jones's former pupils to go through life without a keen enjoyment of music. And the infection might well spread to families and friends. It would help to fill the seats of concert halls and enlarge record collections.

Choir directors, organists, music teachers in grade and high school, professors in college—all these are the Doc Joneses of our lives. May they live long and spread their infectious love of music far and wide!

THREE MUSICIANS >
by Fernand Leger
1944, oil on canvas
Mrs. Simon Guggenheim Fund
Collection, The Museum of
Modern Art
New York

## The Joyful Noise

One of the happiest surprises in a church we know was the recent appearance of a new children's musical group that named themselves "The Joyful Noise." The faces of the more staid members of the congregation took on startled expressions the first two Sundays when the children entered the chancel. What would these smiling, happy children play? What cacophony of sound would they create to break the dignified flow of the liturgy? A blast of rock music? Apprehensive glances were exchanged among some adults, along with smiles at the appearance of this band of children carrying their unconventional (for church!) instruments.

They took their places quickly and without fuss. A member of the adult choir left her place to stand in front of them as conductor. She raised her arms. In almost perfect coordination the instrumentalists began to play the music to the song "They Will Know We Are Christians by Our Love." The junior-aged singers joined the orchestra presently. Tones were sweet, true, and words well enunciated. A second number was a lovely African lullaby.

On the following Sunday their music was more lively. Now, however, they were an acceptable part of the Sunday worship. And why not?

BROADWAY BOOGIE WOOGIE >
by Piet Mondrian
1942-43, oil on canvas
Collection, The Museum of
Modern Art
New York

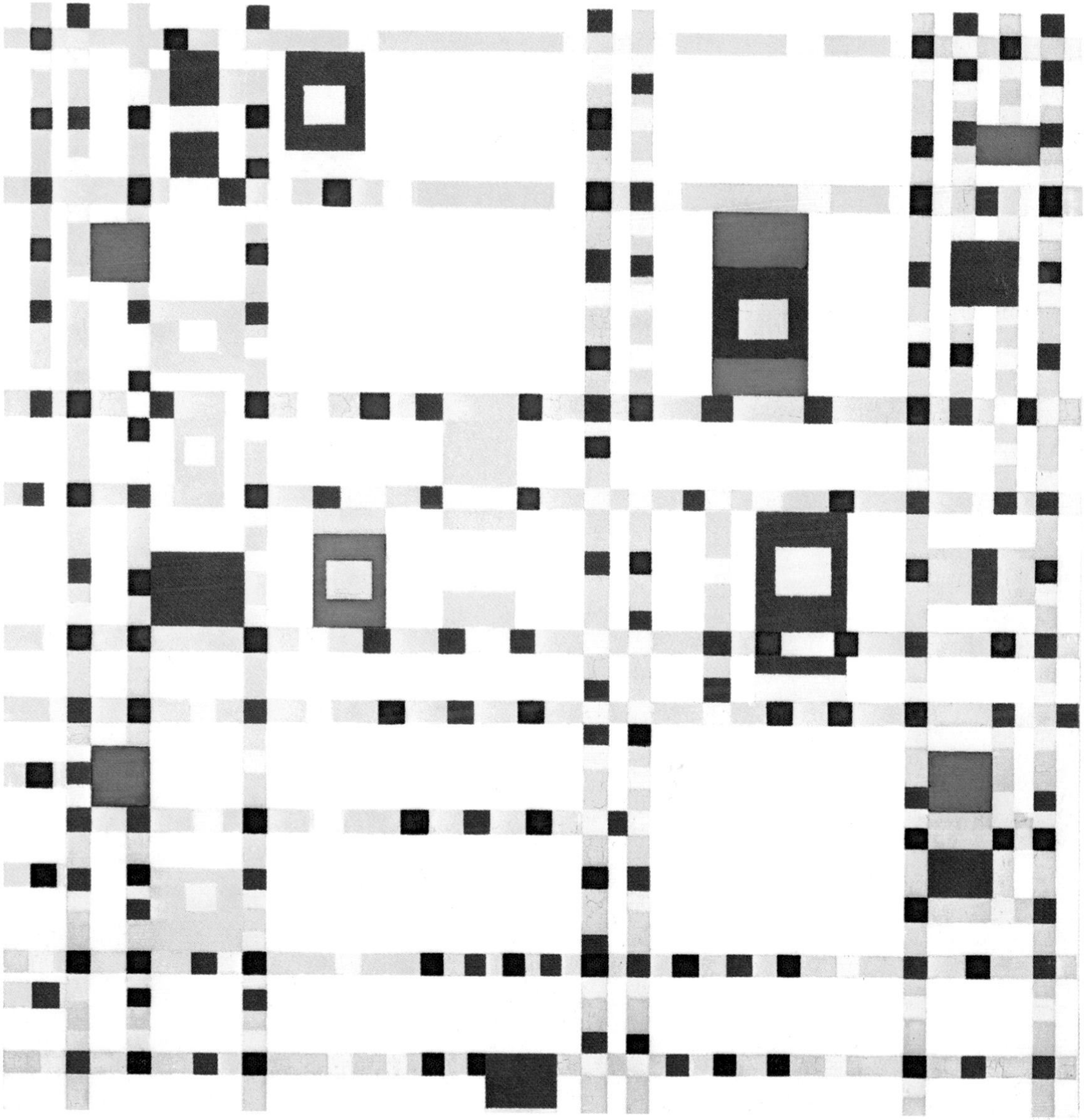

# 4
# COME
# ALIVE

ON THE WATER<
by Mary Cassatt
early 1890's, oil on canvas
Charles H. and Mary F.S.
Worcester Collection
Courtesy, The Art Institute
of Chicago

## Finding Rhythms by Oneself

Between six and seven, an early morning walk in spring and summer can be quite special, even in the city. In town, streets are being cleaned and scrubbed—parks seem fresher, greener, more spic and span in the morning. All-night park-bench sleepers are stirring or taking one last nap. Walking along a river bank, one sees barges and houseboats making their slow, stately way; pilots wave; their wives hang out the washing.

In the country, life goes by the sun, and morning walks need to be earlier than seven o'clock. The world comes alive soon after five!

In the country, the smells are so fresh: dew on fields of hay and clover; woodsy odors of damp pine needles and savory plants. Cheerful are the birds' songs—they have an authority! There are sights to make the eyes open wide: trillium in the woods, white and stately; a rose-pink carpet of creeping phlox. From a hilltop, the valley below is green and lush, cows make their way over pastures toward the barn.

Life in the country stirs early: it is smell, sound, and sight—a feast for the senses!

THE BATHER >
by Paul Cezanne
c. 1885, oil on canvas
Lillie P. Bliss Collection
Collection, The Museum of
Modern Art
New York

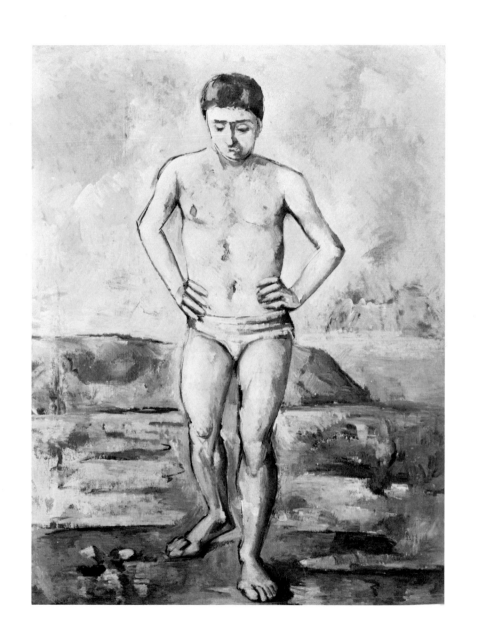

# The Delight of Body Rhythms

The short, slight person who came running up the hill might have been a boy, except that she wore a skirt. She might have been a young girl, except that her hair was gray. Waving gaily, Marjorie drew near, and only when she was a few feet from her friend did she stop, panting lightly and briefly. Marjorie is well past seventy years of age—in fact, she admits to being "about seventy-four."

Walking and running have been a lifelong enjoyment for this New England farm woman. They have kept her figure spare and youthful, her body in prime condition. Marjorie has walked or run all her life—among the flaming maples of autumn, over hills in cross-country snowshoeing, through the apple orchard fragrant with spring blossoms, and in the early morning summer mist.

"I like to go with friends and neighbors, but I like most to go by myself," she says, "because then I can let God help me work out my problems and I usually become calmer and happier. I feel 'in tune'— really alive."

Psychologists say we sense our aliveness when we engage in activities that help us to feel in tune with the rhythms of nature.

Sports, and open-air pastimes such as swimming,

RUNNING GIRL ("LASA") <
Etruscan
early fifth century B.C., bronze
H. L. Pierce Fund
Courtesy, Museum of Fine Arts
Boston

walking, bicycling, skiing, sailing, rowing, canoeing, or even raking leaves, are excellent for body and spirit. Prisoners testify that one of the most difficult things about confinement is being deprived of complete freedom of motion. To walk and swing along in the open is not only good exercise, but it brings the joy of being part of nature, of feeling released and really free.

To walk in the light of a full moon is a marvelous experience! The night brightness of the sky is enhanced by stars and often there are billowing clouds that drift by fast or slowly, depending on the wind. If the moon is bright, it casts shadows on the ground, and at times one can actually see to read by moonlight. Branches of trees are lovely against the night sky. It is good to lie on the ground and look up at the stars, or to climb to the top of a hill and sense their closeness.

Marjorie and others like her who walk in the out-of-doors know full well the delight of body rhythms. In all kinds of weather, at any time of day or night, walking has rich rewards!

DANCING GIRL >
by Paul Klee
Swiss, 1940, oil on linen glued
to panel
Gift of Mr. George B. Young
Courtesy, The Art Institute
of Chicago

We are unwilling walkers. We are not innocent and simple-hearted enough to enjoy a walk. . . . He who marvels at the beauty of the world in summer will find equal cause for wonder and admiration in the winter. . . . Look at the miracle of falling snow— the air a dizzy maze of whirling, eddying flakes, noiselessly transforming the world, the exquisite crystals dropping in ditch and gutter, and disguising in the same suit of spotless livery all objects on which they fall. . . . All life and action upon the snow have an added emphasis and significance. Every expression is underscored. . . . All sounds are sharper in winter; the air transmits better. . . . The world lies about me in a trance of snow. The clouds are pearly and iridescent. . . . I see the hills, bulging with great drifts, lift themselves up cold and white against the sky. . . . At this season Nature makes the most of every throb of life that can withstand her severity.

WINTER SUNSHINE >
by John Burroughs
excerpt

72

Mr. George Barker, of Wood Green, celebrated his ninetieth birthday yesterday by his customary annual walk of 18 miles to St. Albans. Starting at 6 o'clock yesterday morning he reached St. Albans at 1 p.m., strictly to his schedule for the past 20 years, although he broke his non-stop record by two halts because a nail in his shoe pressed against a toe. On returning home, he took part in a family celebration and played the violin and recited poetry of his own composition.

THE LONDON TIMES <
May 1, 1933
item

*To Be Alive*

is to feel wind in your hair and know it's *there*; to feel sun on your back, warm, relaxing. It is to feel muscles tense and then settle into rhythm when the body is in motion.

*To Be Alive*

is to look at a sunrise or sunset on a lake, mountain, or over city roofs and let its glory take hold of you— shake and shape you for the moment or more. It is to see a rose-breasted grosbeak, a scarlet tanager, or a weed like Queen Anne's lace and marvel at its beauty. This is to be alive! It's more too—

*To Be Alive*

is to quicken at another's glance, at the touch of a hand, a kiss. It is to sense that someone loves you— cares enough to enjoy being near. It is to reach out— to be caught up in the life of the world you live in and know you are not really living unless you are involved. Being alive is complicated; it is so much more than breathing, heartbeat, and blood circulation. It's you and the world, with God there somehow, helping to make sense, meaning, and value out of it all.

74

PULSE>
by Robert Vickrey
tempera
Collection of Randolph-Macon
Woman's College
Courtesy, Midtown Galleries
New York

## Dancers All

We dance in many ways: whenever we are in bodily rhythm with others, as when we play tennis, handball, basketball, volleyball, football.

What is more swift and graceful than a group of racing downhill skiers in the intricacies of a swaying, zigzag slalom race? Or skaters moving skillfully and speedily over an ice rink? A spectator is moved to excitement on seeing rowers in a scull, skimming down a river in perfect rhythm, or watching a football game or a tennis match.

The real dancers, though—they are the rhythm-makers *par excellence*! A troupe of Russian dancers performing their vigorous footwork inspired the painting "Rhythm of a Russian Dance" by van Doesburg. All of the dancers' rhythm was translated by this artist's brush into patterned lines set at right angles to each other. That was how the dancers seemed to this artist. Another artist might show a dancing girl in wild rhythm—arms stretched out so far that to communicate this farness, he would extend their length out of proportion.

These, then, are the dancers—rhythmic in body, feeling the pulse of life and translating it into bodily movement.

RHYTHM OF A RUSSIAN
DANCE<
by Theo. Van Doesburg
1918, oil on canvas
Acquired through the Lillie P.
Bliss Bequest
Collection, The Museum of
Modern Art
New York

77

With lifted feet, hands still,
I am poised, and down the hill
Dart, with heedful mind;
The air goes by in a wind.

Swifter and yet more swift,
Till the heart with a mighty lift
Makes the lungs laugh, the throat cry:—
"O bird, see; see, bird, I fly.

"Is this, is this your joy?
O bird, then, I, though a boy,
For a golden moment share
Your feathery life in air!"

"GOING DOWN HILL ON
A BICYCLE"<
by Henry Charles Beeching
excerpts

THE DAIRY RUN>
by Robert Vickrey
tempera
Courtesy, Midtown Galleries
New York

78

# 5
# FULFILLMENT

SANDSPIT <
by Andrew Wyeth
tempera on masonite
Bequest of Lillian Oakley Beebe
Courtesy, Museum of Fine Arts
Boston

## Fulfillment

Finding one's way in the world could be compared to walking along a road or path. Sometimes the way is straight; other times it curves and climbs. One walks on steppingstones or crosses bridges. Sometimes one walks with another person or with several others. Frequently, one walks alone. Under any circumstances, the walk through life is a personal journey, for each must find his own way and come to the realization of who he is and where he is going.

How does one describe the state of being "fulfilled"? What, indeed, is a fulfilled person? Unfortunately there are no set norms that a person can look to and, having reached those standards, know that he has arrived. Like the figure in Andrew Wyeth's painting "Sandspit," each of us dreams his or her own dreams and finds a way to fulfillment. To realize that one is well on the way to this is to take more joy—the kind of joy that is love both received and poured out.

STEPPING STONES >
by Mirtala Bentov
bronze
Courtesy, Pucker/Safrai Gallery
Boston

82

# Patchwork and Design

"Patchwork Quilt," a collage by Romare Bearden, is an odd piece, not easy to understand. Like most contemporary artists, Bearden would probably reply to the question, "What does it mean?" by asking another question, "What do *you* think it means?"

So try taking off from there.

A collage is made of bits and pieces arranged in a design that is pleasing to its creator. Bearden did his collage with cloth and paper, using synthetic polymer paint and arranging these on a composition board. He did it large: three feet by four feet. Four kinds of materials, very old and very new, were brought together to form a unit with a stylized figure standing or stretched out on a patchwork quilt.

What pulls the design together to give it unity? The figure which is suggestively Egyptian? Or is it the quilt? Perhaps both, if you sense that it takes the figure *and* the patchwork background to make this a finished unit. Each part is complete in itself, but both are blended to make a larger whole.

A good and satisfying life is like that: made up of patchwork, with ourselves set against these fragments and stretches of time and events. Some of the patches are as joyous as flowers, plaids, and polka-

PATCHWORK QUILT >
by Romare Bearden
1970, collage
Blanchette Rockefeller Fund
Collection, The Museum of
Modern Art
New York

dots; others are dull and repetitious, like stripes or plain material.

An enigmatic work of contemporary art such as "Patchwork Quilt" becomes a "think piece," requiring imagination and free-wheeling thought to be appreciated.

## The Butterfly Net

On a brick-red path that runs through a bright green lawn stands a boy with a butterfly net. This redheaded, sandaled boy has a thoughtful look that goes with his hesitant pose. He seems to be thinking, wondering, perhaps planning his next move: where and how to catch a butterfly.

Butterflies are not easy to catch. Those colorful, gorgeous creatures flit and dip to elude the net. Because they are short-lived and distinctively colored and patterned, they are not so much for keeping as to be held for a moment of admiration and wonder and then released to fly free.

To take more joy in a world like ours requires something of the makeup of the butterfly-catcher, who captures beauty when and where he finds it, takes from it the sheer joy of the moment, then lets it go—glad for the experience alone.

BOY WITH BUTTERFLY NET <
by Henri Matisse
French, 1869-1954
The John R. Van Derlip Fund
Courtesy, The Minneapolis Institute
of Arts

87

He who binds to himself a Joy
Doth the winged life destroy;
But he who kisses the Joy as it flies
Lives in Eternity's sun-rise.

"LIBERTY">
by William Blake
excerpt

THE BASKERVILLE ROCK<
by Robert Vickrey
1972, tempera
Courtesy, Midtown Galleries
New York

Here in this quiet place
Where beeches grow
A century tall, where time
Slows down at the bend of the brook,
I let myself uncoil
Like the tight-wound fronds
Of waking ferns. The songs
Of warblers darting among
The burgeoning leaves
Translate the silence, while
Thousands of golden-belled
Dogtooth violets
Interpret the hillside hush.

"THIS QUIET PLACE">
by John Robert Quinn
Reprinted by permission from
The Christian Science Monitor
© 1973, The Christian Science
Publishing Society
All rights reserved.

90

Give me my scallop-shell of quiet,
My staff of faith to walk upon,
My scrip of joy, immortal diet,
My bottle of salvation,
My gown of glory, hope's true gage,
And thus I'll take my pilgrimage.                    by Sir Walter Raleigh <

## Reminders of Love

Some children we know made "love cubes" to remind themselves and others of the presence of love. They covered several boxes of a uniform size with gaily colored fabric or paper. From contrasting material they cut out the large letters LOVE to paste on the surfaces of the boxes. Using nylon thread, they suspended the love cubes from the ceilings of the corridors of their church, and the kitchens and recreation rooms of their homes.

Another group of young people created "love mobiles" with cutouts of symbols that reminded them of love: hearts, hands, doves.

Children can make reminders of love like these for church and home. They could also give them to patients in a nursing home. In delivering the mobiles to the home, they would further express their love by singing songs for the patients.

BOY <
by Bernard Karfiol
oil on canvas
The Phillips Collection
Washington, D.C.

93

# Perfect Joy

Francis of Assisi's "Canticle of the Creatures"—or "Canticle of the Sun," as it is frequently called—is so often quoted, sung, paraphrased, and pictured that it has become, perhaps, the favorite writing attributed to the saint. Not so familiar is his little sermon on "Perfect Joy."

It seems that one bitterly cold day, when Francis and Friar Leo were walking, Francis began to think about joy. He asked Friar Leo to write down his thoughts as he spoke them aloud.

Francis spoke first about what joy is *not*. Perfect joy is not found in scholarship or knowledge, he said; it is not given to those who work miracles, or who know all about birds, fishes, stones, waters. Nor, said Francis, is perfect joy to be found in great preaching.

For two miles, Francis preached to Friar Leo about what joy is *not*. Finally Friar Leo had had enough and he turned to Francis saying, "In God's name, tell me where perfect joy is to be found!"

With what may well have been a bit of humor, Francis described how the two of them would be arriving at their destination, cold and hungry. If the lodge-keeper angrily turned them away, abused, cold, and hungry, and called them all manner of foul

SAINT FRANCIS IN ECSTASY >
by Giovanni Bellini
1430?-1516
Courtesy, The Frick Collection
New York

names—if this should happen and the two men were to endure it patiently for the love of Christ, then they would know perfect joy.

The story as it is usually told ends here, but there is more to it; and to stop short is to leave out the real point, for Francis continues:

"And now, Friar Leo, hear the conclusion. Above all the grace and gifts of the Holy Spirit that Christ giveth to His beloved is that of overcoming self, and for the love of Him willingly to bear pain and buffetings and revilings and discomforts; for in none other of God's gifts, save these, may we glory, seeing they are not ours but of God."

Seek ye the kingdom of God; and all these things shall be added unto you.

LUKE 12:31 <

OVER VITEBSK >
by Marc Chagall
1915-20, oil on canvas
Acquired through the Lillie P.
Bliss Bequest
Collection, The Museum of
Modern Art
New York

## Practicing Love

For several years people in a certain church have followed a formula for practicing love during the Lenten season. It is a spiritual exercise that could be used any time of the year to help make one more aware of ways to extend love among persons. It runs like this:

Every day the *hand of love* will write a letter to a friend. The writer of the letter will include some expression of appreciation for the friendship.

Everyday the *voice of love* will telephone at least one person for a brief "Thank you," "I'm sorry," "How are you?" or "Congratulations." When these calls go to persons not usually telephoned, they will be pleasantly surprised.

A *work of love* will be planned for at least one person who is seldom or never remembered by others. This may be an invitation to go for an automobile ride, the gift of a small jar of homemade marmalade or jelly, cookies, or a loaf of bread. Other works of love, asking for nothing in return, might be the offer of a helping hand with some chore or the loan of a book or phonograph records.

*Prayers of love* will include praying and thinking about a number of special people each day, not

THE PICTURE BOOK
(STORYBOOK) <
by Gertrude Kasebier
1902, Platinum print
Gift of Mrs. Hermine Turner
Collection, The Museum of Modern
Art
New York

all of whom may be well-liked. Willingness to forgive will grow with prayer!

The *mind of love* will look inward and face inadequacies, name fears, and give thanks for strength to live.

A *celebration of love* is sure to come as God's love is realized and felt through appreciation of his created world of nature and persons. The celebration may take the form of a picnic, party, or a time of joyous worship when faith, hope, and love are acknowledged.

## Be Thou my Vision

Be Thou my vision, O Lord of my heart
Naught is all else to me, save that Thou art.

Thou my best thought by day and by night,
Waking or sleeping, Thy presence my light.

Be Thou my wisdom, Thou my true word:
I ever with Thee, Thou with me, Lord.

Thou my great father, I Thy dear son;
Thou in my dwelling. I with Thee one.

Be Thou my battle-shield, sword for the fight,
Be Thou my dignity, Thou my delight.

Author Unknown <
eighth century
translated by Eleanor Hull
from *1,000 Years of Irish Poetry*
Devin Adair Company

COURAGE OF FULL VISION >
by Mirtala Bentov
bronze
Courtesy, Pucker/Safrai Gallery
Boston

100

Thou my soul's shelter, Thou my high tower;
Raise Thou me heavenward, power of my power.

Riches I heed not, nor man's empty praise,
Thou mine inheritance now and always.

Thou, and Thou only, first in my heart,
High king of heaven, my treasure Thou art.

King of the seven heavens, grant me for dole,
Thy love in my heart, Thy light in my soul.

Thy light from my soul, Thy love from my heart,
King of the seven heavens, may they never depart.

With the high king of heaven, after victory won,
May I reach heaven's joys, O bright heaven's sun!

Heart of my own heart, whatever befall,
Still be my vision, O Ruler of all.